How Your Body Works

A Good Look
Inside
Your Insides

Illustrated by
Carolyn Franklin

Written by
David Stewart

Hold the page
up to the light
and see if you
can see the
skeletons.

children's press®
An Imprint of Scholastic Inc.
NEW YORK • TORONTO • LONDON • AUCKLAND • SYDNEY
MEXICO CITY • NEW DELHI • HONG KONG
DANBURY, CONNECTICUT

ISBN-13: 978-0-531-20444-3 (lib. bdg.)   978-0-531-20455-9 (pbk.)
ISBN-10: 0-531-20444-8 (lib. bdg.)   0-531-20455-3 (pbk.)

Published in 2008 in the United States
by Children's Press, an imprint of Scholastic Inc.,
557 Broadway, New York, NY 10012.

A CIP catalog record for this book is available
from the Library of Congress.

Author: David Stewart has written many nonfiction books for children on historical topics, including *You Wouldn't Want to be an Egyptian Mummy!* and *You Wouldn't Want to Sail on the Titanic!* He lives in Brighton, England, with his wife and son.

Artist: Carolyn Franklin is a graduate of Brighton College of Art, England, specializing in design and illustration. She has worked in animation, advertising, and children's fiction and nonfiction. She has a special interest in natural history and has written many books on the subject including *Life in the Wetlands* in the WHAT ON EARTH? series and *Egg to Owl* in the CYCLES OF LIFE series.

Consultant: Monica Hughes is an experienced Educational Advisor and author of more than one hundred books for young children. She has been headteacher of a primary school, primary advisory teacher and senior lecturer in early childhood education.

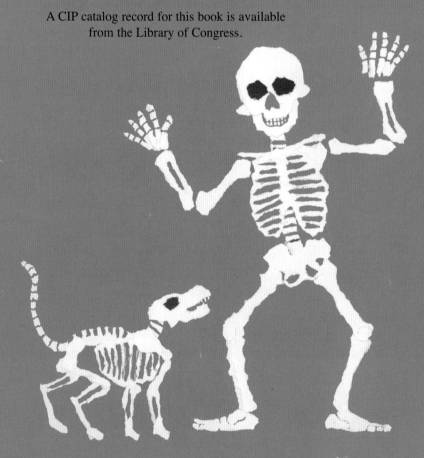

Printed and bound in China.
Printed on paper from sustainable sources.

Contents

Introduction

You may look different from your best friend on the outside, but inside you are the same. The inside of your body is the same as that of your parents, your friends, and everyone else in the world.

Look at the faces below. Can you see what makes each face look different and what makes them look the same?

There are many different skin colors and hair colors. But everybody has two eyes, a nose, and a mouth.

Try making these faces in a mirror.

Happy   RUde   Sad   Surprised

Inside your body is a skeleton like the one in this picture. Everyone has a skeleton and every skeleton has the same parts.

How Do I Taste and Smell Things?

Taste and smell are just two of your body's senses. They work together to send signals to your brain. Your senses of smell and taste can warn you of danger. You can smell if something is on fire. You can taste if food is spoiled and might make you sick.

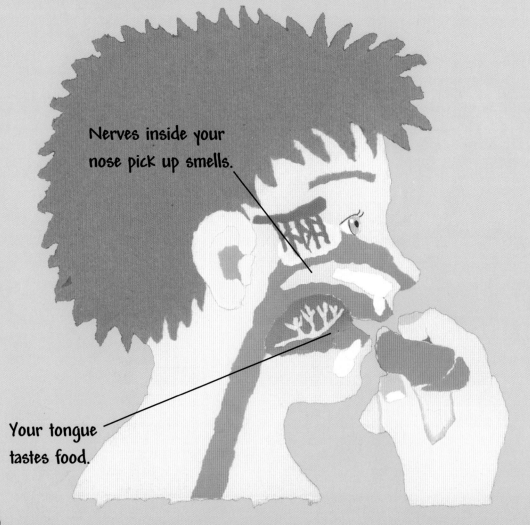

Nerves inside your nose pick up smells.

Your tongue tastes food.

Your tongue is covered with thousands of tiny **taste buds** that identify the different tastes in foods and drinks.

Different areas of your tongue taste different things.

Tastes can be bitter, sweet, salty, or sour.

bitter tastes at the back

sour tastes in the middle

salty and sweet tastes at the front

Five senses

Your body has senses of touch, taste, smell, sight, and hearing.

It is harder to recognize tastes if you cannot see the food!

7

How Do I Hear and See?

Most of your ear is inside your head and you cannot see it. The part of the ear you can see is like a funnel for sounds.

When sound reaches your **eardrum** inside, it vibrates.

nerves

eardrum

Vroom

Meeow!

Splash! Bang! Toot toot!

Crash! Woof!

As your eardrum vibrates, it sends messages to your brain that make sense of what you are hearing.

You see with your eyes. Light passes through your eye to a part called the **retina** at the back of your eye. Your retina sends the image of what you see to your brain.

The colored part of your eye is called the iris.
Your pupil is the black hole that lets light into your eye.

Seeing is believing?

The picture on your retina is upside down. Your brain then figures out how it should look.

iris

pupil

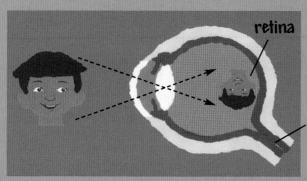

retina

Your optic nerve carries messages to your brain.

Why Do I Have Teeth?

You have teeth so that you can break down your food before you swallow it. Your first set of teeth are called **baby teeth**. Your baby teeth gradually fall out and bigger adult teeth grow in their place.

Children have 20 baby teeth. Adults have 32 teeth. How many do you have? Count them and see.

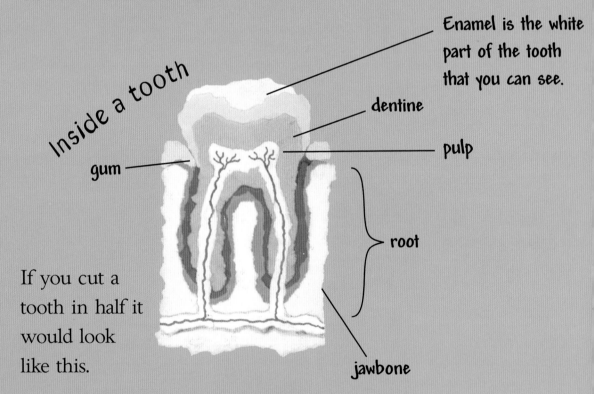

Inside a tooth

Enamel is the white part of the tooth that you can see.

dentine

gum

pulp

root

If you cut a tooth in half it would look like this.

jawbone

You have different teeth for different uses. At the front of your mouth are **incisors** and **canines** for biting and tearing your food. At the back are big teeth called **molars** that crush and grind food.

Molars crush and grind.

Canines are for tearing.

Incisors are sharp for biting.

Hold the page up to the light to see the skeleton.

Why Do I Have Bones?

You have 206 bones in your body. Each one has a different job to do. Bones make up your skeleton, which is what gives your body its shape.

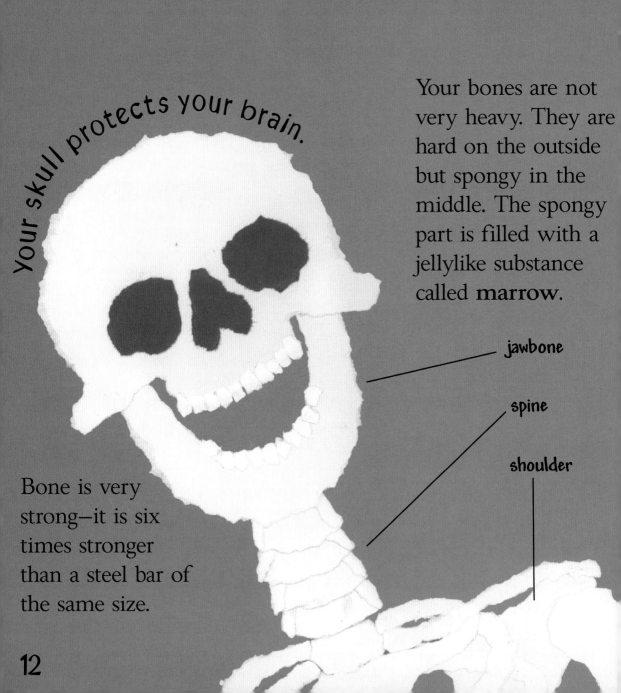

Your skull protects your brain.

Your bones are not very heavy. They are hard on the outside but spongy in the middle. The spongy part is filled with a jellylike substance called **marrow**.

jawbone

spine

shoulder

Bone is very strong—it is six times stronger than a steel bar of the same size.

Joints

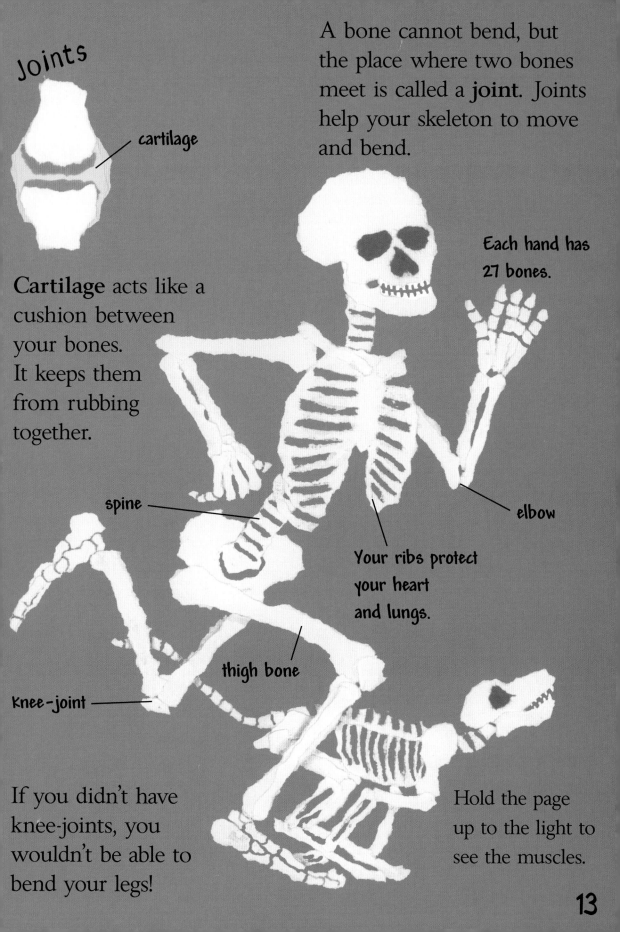

cartilage

A bone cannot bend, but the place where two bones meet is called a **joint**. Joints help your skeleton to move and bend.

Each hand has 27 bones.

Cartilage acts like a cushion between your bones. It keeps them from rubbing together.

spine

elbow

Your ribs protect your heart and lungs.

thigh bone

Knee-joint

If you didn't have knee-joints, you wouldn't be able to bend your legs!

Hold the page up to the light to see the muscles.

13

Why Do I Have Muscles?

You have muscles all over your body and they help you move. When you run, it is your muscles that lift and push each leg forward.

Your biggest muscle is in your bottom!

Muscles are fastened to your bones by strong cords called **tendons.**

Your Achilles tendon is the biggest tendon in your body.

14

Most muscles work in pairs. As one muscle gets shorter, the other muscle gets longer.

This muscle (the biceps) gets shorter when you bend your arm.

Try it for yourself. Hold out your arm and feel the big muscle (the biceps) on the top part of your arm. As you bend your arm upwards, you can feel this muscle getting harder and bigger as it gets shorter.

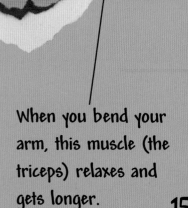

When you bend your arm, this muscle (the triceps) relaxes and gets longer.

15

Why Do I Have Skin?

Your skin covers your body and protects it. It helps to keep your "insides" in, and keeps dirt and water out. It grows with you and it mends itself if you fall and skin your knees.

Your skin grows with you—it will always be a perfect fit.

Not everyone's skin is the same color. Also, some parts of your body have softer skin than others. Skin has **pores**—very small holes that let sweat out when your body gets too hot.

This close-up picture shows
what you would see if you
could look under your skin.

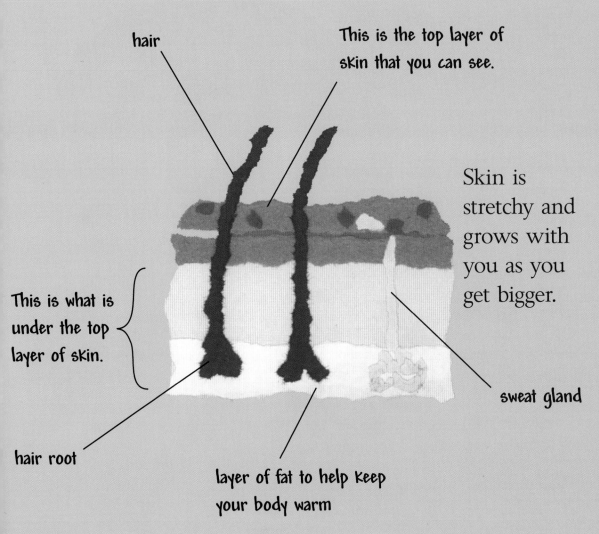

hair

This is the top layer of
skin that you can see.

Skin is
stretchy and
grows with
you as you
get bigger.

This is what is
under the top
layer of skin.

sweat gland

hair root

layer of fat to help keep
your body warm

Tiny hairs grow all over your
skin, except on your lips, the
palms of your hands, and the
soles of your feet.

How Does My Stomach Work?

When you bite into an apple, your teeth break it up into small pieces. As you swallow, these pieces slip down your foodpipe into your stomach.

Eat an apple

Food gives your body energy.

foodpipe

You chew food with your teeth before you swallow it.

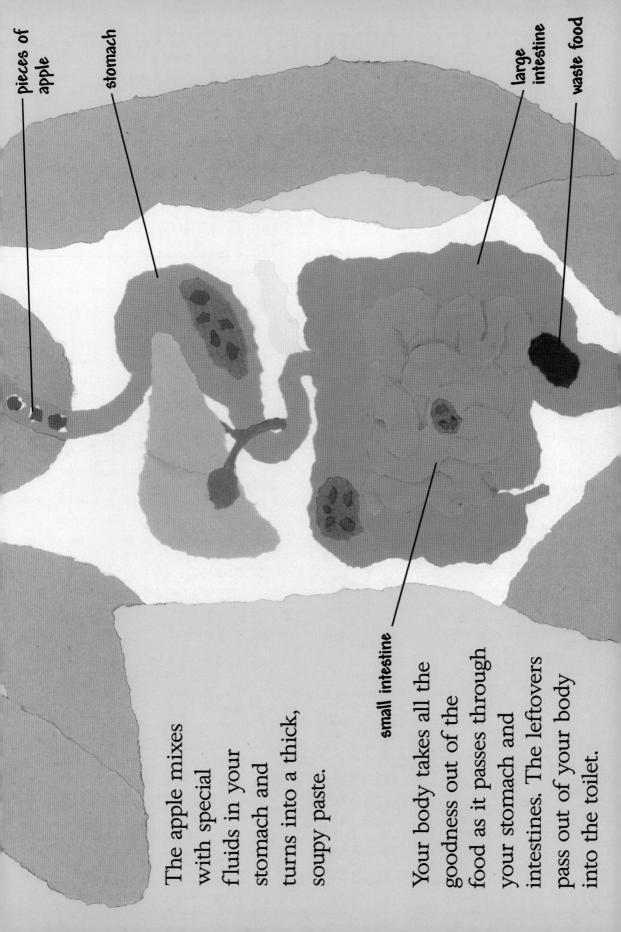

pieces of apple

stomach

large intestine

waste food

small intestine

The apple mixes with special fluids in your stomach and turns into a thick, soupy paste.

Your body takes all the goodness out of the food as it passes through your stomach and intestines. The leftovers pass out of your body into the toilet.

What Do My Lungs Do?

You need lungs to breathe. Your lungs supply your body with life-giving air. Without air, you would die.

You can breathe through your nose or your mouth. Air goes down your **windpipe** into your lungs.

Air contains **oxygen.** As you breathe air into your lungs, oxygen is sent into your bloodstream.

lungs

windpipe

Air passages inside your lungs are like the branches of an upside-down tree.

breathe **in**
oxygen

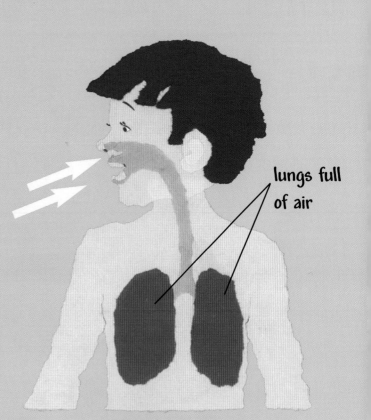

You need oxygen to live. As you breathe in, your lungs fill up with oxygen-rich air. The air passages in your lungs take the oxygen into your body.

lungs full of air

breathe **out**
carbon dioxide

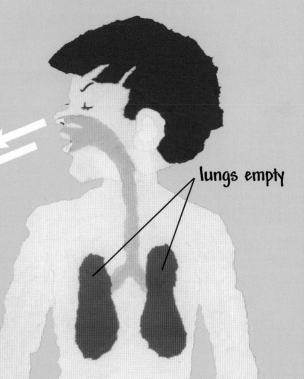

lungs empty

The air that you breathe out is called **carbon dioxide**. As you breathe out, your body gets rid of unwanted carbon dioxide.

What Do My Kidneys Do?

You have two kidneys that clean your blood. They get rid of the things your body doesn't need. This waste liquid is called **urine**.

About two pints of blood flow through your kidneys every minute.

Urine travels from your kidneys and fills up your bladder. It passes out of your body into the toilet.

You have one bean-shaped kidney on the left and one on the right side of your body.

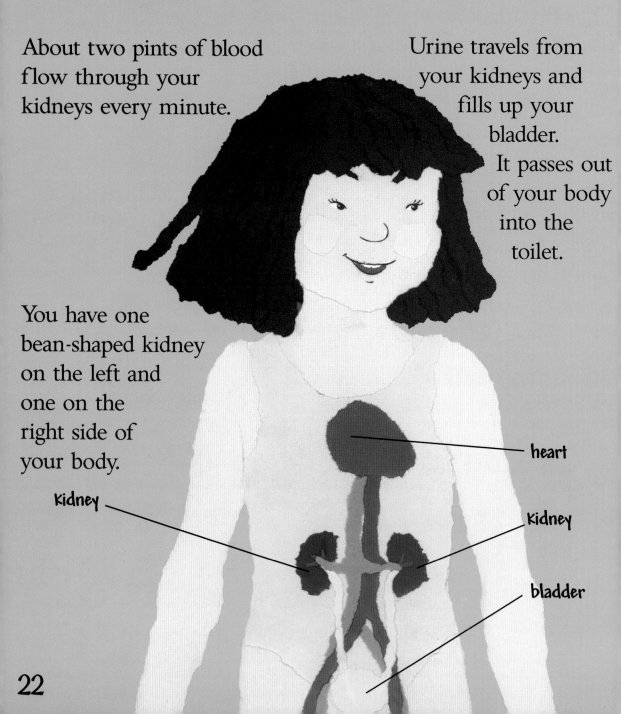

kidney

heart

kidney

bladder

What Does My Liver Do?

Your liver does many different things. It makes a special fluid called **bile**. Bile helps to break down fat and old blood cells.

Your liver and kidneys help to make vitamin D, which makes your bones stronger.

Your liver also makes and stores some **vitamins**. It takes **toxins** out of your blood.

Your liver is quite big. It is about the size of a grapefruit!

liver

What Does My Heart Do?

Your heart is a muscle. It is about the size of your clenched fist. Your heart pumps blood to every part of your body. The blood is pumped through **arteries** and **veins**.

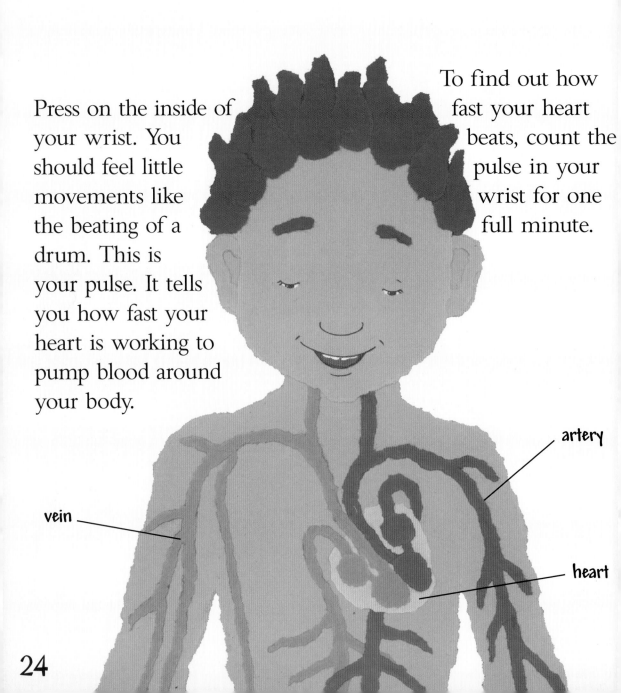

Press on the inside of your wrist. You should feel little movements like the beating of a drum. This is your pulse. It tells you how fast your heart is working to pump blood around your body.

To find out how fast your heart beats, count the pulse in your wrist for one full minute.

artery

vein

heart

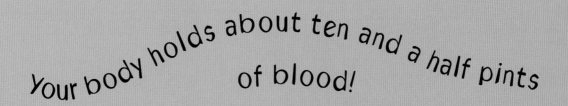

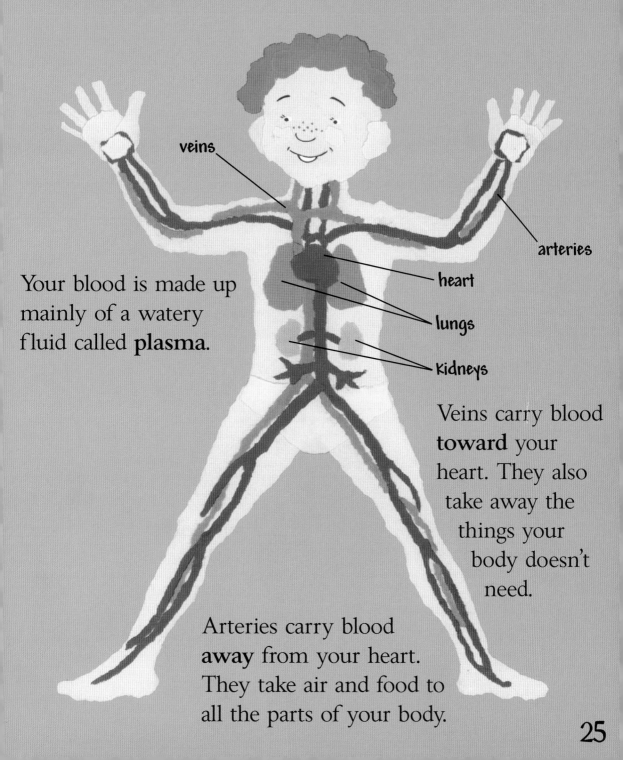

veins

arteries

heart

lungs

kidneys

Your blood is made up mainly of a watery fluid called **plasma**.

Veins carry blood **toward** your heart. They also take away the things your body doesn't need.

Arteries carry blood **away** from your heart. They take air and food to all the parts of your body.

25

How Does My Brain Work?

Your brain is inside your skull. It is your body's computer. Your brain gets messages from around your body and decides what to do. It controls your thoughts, movements, and memory.

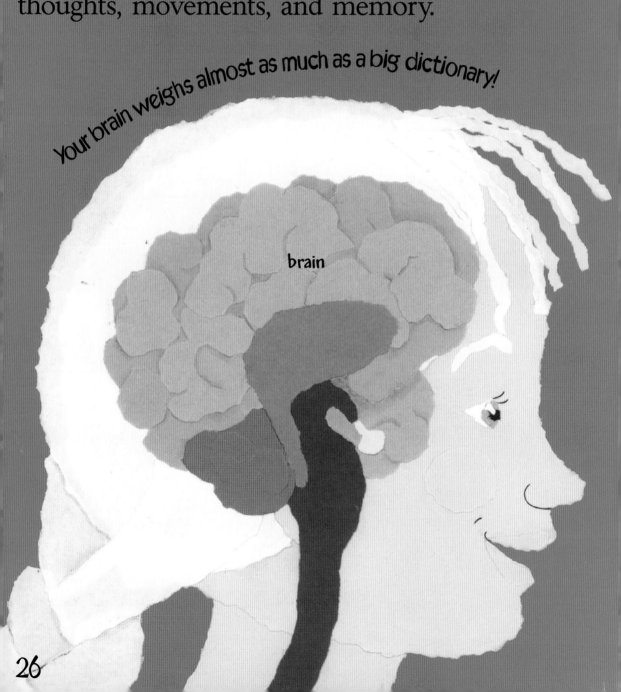

Your brain weighs almost as much as a big dictionary!

brain

When you see a ball in the air, your brain sends a message down your **spinal cord** to your **nerves**. Your nerves then send a message to your muscles to help you move and catch the ball. This takes much less than a second!

You have nerves all over your body sending all kinds of messages to your brain.

Your **spinal cord** carries messages to your brain from every nerve in your body.

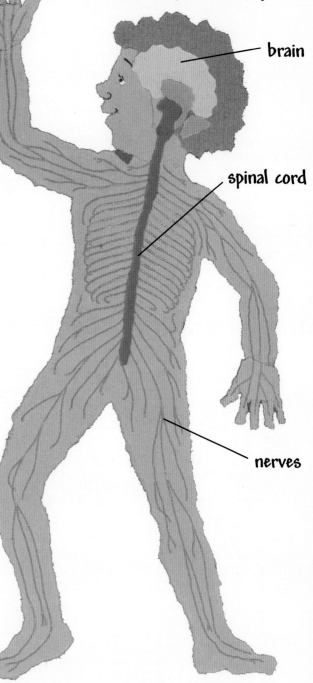

brain

spinal cord

nerves

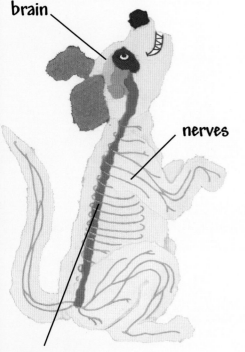

brain

nerves

spinal cord

27

Things to Do

Feel the chill!

You will need:
Two glasses
Six ice cubes
Lard or solid vegetable
    shortening
Cold water

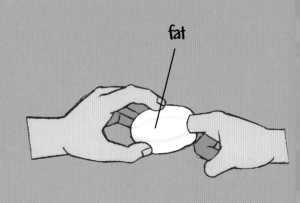

fat

1   Fill two glasses with water and put three ice cubes in each one.

2   Shape the fat into a ball. Carefully push one finger into the middle of the ball. Make sure your finger is completely covered by the fat.

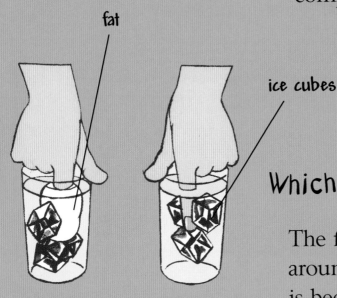

fat

ice cubes

3   Put a finger in each glass of water.

Which finger feels coldest?

The finger with the fat around it feels warmer! This is because the fat prevents the skin on your finger from feeling cold. The fat inside your body helps to keep you warm in the same way.

Seeing stars!

You will need:
A 3-inch piece of cardboard
2 20-inch pieces of yarn
1 red and 1 blue marker
Scissors

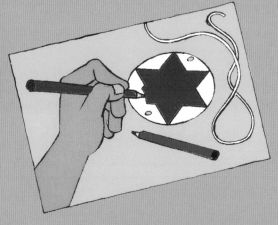

3   Make a small hole on either side of the cardboard and thread a loop of yarn through each hole.

4   Put each loop around your thumb and forefinger and swing the circle round several times. When the yarn is twisted tight, pull it in and out to make it spin.

1   Ask an adult to help you cut the cardboard into a circle 3 inches in diameter. Draw a large star on one side of the card and color it red.

2   Turn the cardboard over and draw a small circle in the center. Color it blue.

What do you see?

29

More Things to Do

You will need:
3 feet of plastic tubing
Plastic funnel
A friend

Listen to your friend's heart!

2   Ask your friend to put the open end of the funnel on the middle of his or her chest.

3   Put the other end of the tube to your ear.

1   Ask an adult to push the narrow end of the funnel into one end of the tubing.

What can you hear?

Words to Remember

Bile A liquid made by your liver that helps to break down food.

Bladder A bag inside your body that holds urine until you go to the toilet.

Eardrum The part of your ear that vibrates when you hear sounds.

Intestines These long tubes help to digest food, absorb it into the body, and get rid of waste.

Nerves Bundles of fibers that carry messages from different parts of your body to your brain.

Retina The part of your eye that responds to light. Your retina uses the optic nerve to pass messages to your brain about what you can see.

Senses The parts of the body that tell us what the outside world smells, sounds, feels, tastes, and looks like.

Spine The long row of small bones that runs from the bottom of your back to the top of your neck.

Toxins Waste substances made by your body as it digests food and drink.

Vitamins Special substances found in food. You need vitamins to keep you healthy.

Index